MCR

EVANSTON PUBLIC LIBRARY

3 1192 01426 9417

x398.45 Ayles.T
Aylesworth, Thomas G.
Vampires and other ghosts

D1566158

VAMPIRES
and Other Ghosts

*To Ray Broekel,
who claims to have been a college roommate
of Count Dracula*

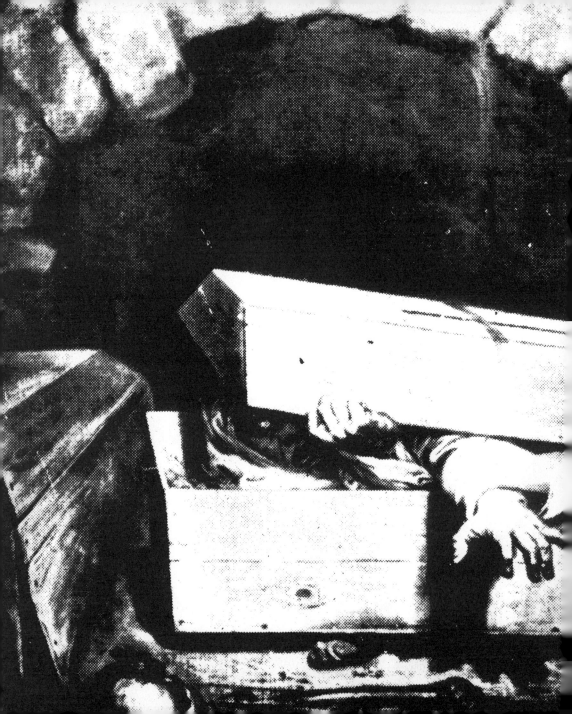

CHOLERA

EVANSTON PUBLIC LIBRARY
CHILDREN'S DEPARTMENT
1703 ORRINGTON AVENUE
EVANSTON, ILLINOIS 60201

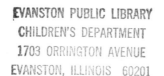

Vampires
and Other
Ghosts

THOMAS G. AYLESWORTH

 Addison-Wesley

Addisonian Press titles
by Thomas G. Aylesworth
SERVANTS OF THE DEVIL
WEREWOLVES AND OTHER MONSTERS
VAMPIRES AND OTHER GHOSTS

 An Addisonian Press Book

Text copyright © 1972 by Thomas G. Aylesworth
Illustrations copyright © 1972 by Addison-Wesley
Publishing Company, Inc.
All Rights Reserved
Addison-Wesley Publishing Company, Inc.
Reading, Massachusetts 01867
Printed in the United States of America

Library of Congress Cataloging in Publication Data
Aylesworth, Thomas G.
  Vampires and other ghosts.
  SUMMARY: Presents lore and myths from various
parts of the world about vampires, zombies, and other
supernatural creatures and examines their basis in
actual events.
  1. Vampires—Juvenile literature. 2. Ghosts
—Juvenile literature. [1. Vampires. 2. Ghosts]
I. Title.
BF1556.A9   398.4'5   76–39296
ISBN 0–201–00157–8

CONTENTS

INTRODUCTION / There aren't any haunted houses in this book. Nor are there invisible spirits, poltergeists, or seances. The only things that you will find here are the kinds of ghosts that you can see (if you are a believer) and that can see you.

There is no room in this book for explanations about the ancient art of spiritualism, or of mediums, or of studies concerning extra-sensory perception. This would require many volumes.

There could be an argument about the statement that a vampire is a ghost. Some people would claim that the vampire and the zombie, while certainly not alive, are also not dead. They are un-dead. But I take the view, as do others, that they were alive at one time, died, and then came back to take advantage of human beings.

Perhaps there are some reasonable explanations for what is found on these pages. Perhaps not. You will find some scientific data on a few incidents, but not too much.

On the other hand, you may just *want* to believe in vampires and other ghosts; that's your privilege, many people do.

One definition—a ghost is a dead person who appears to be still alive. So that eliminates demons and devils, since they never were alive. And it also eliminates monsters and witches, since they are not dead yet.

But let's get on with the story.

Thomas G. Aylesworth
Stamford, Connecticut
Dracula's Birthday, 1972

THE VAMPIRE

ONE / WITH SHARP WHITE TEETH / Is
this man a friend of yours?

"His face was a strong—a very strong—aquiline, with
high bridge of the thin nose and peculiarly arched nostrils; with lofty domed forehead, and hair growing
scantily around the temples but profusely elsewhere.
His eyebrows were very massive, almost meeting over
the nose, and with bushy hair that seemed to curl in its
own profusion. The mouth, so far as I could see it under
the heavy moustache, was fixed and rather cruel-looking,
with peculiarly sharp white teeth; these protruded over
the lips, whose remarkable ruddiness showed astonish-
ing vitality in a man of his years. For the rest, his ears
were pale, and at tops extremely pointed; the chin was
broad and strong, and the cheeks firm though thin. The
general effect was one of extraordinary pallor.

"Hitherto I had noticed the backs of his hands . . . and
they had seemed rather white and fine; but seeing them

The greatest of all
movie vampires, Bela Lugosi,
is shown in a scene from
the 1931 Universal picture, *Dracula.*

now close to me, I could not but notice that they were rather coarse — broad, with squat fingers . . . there were hairs in the center of the palm. The nails were long and fine, and cut to a sharp point."

This is a description of the main character in the novel *Dracula,* by Bram Stoker. And the weird creature is a vampire.

According to ancient beliefs, a vampire is a ghost who comes up out of his grave and wanders about all night. On his journeys he sucks the blood of humans. As a result the victims usually die and become vampires themselves.

Sometimes these horrible creatures are called ghouls, although that is not an accurate name for them. The ghoul was an Arabic demon who fed on corpses or small children. It lived in deserts, lonely places, or graveyards. But supposedly it had never been alive, so it could not have been a real vampire.

The belief in vampires goes back a long way — at least to ancient Greece. Perhaps the legend began with the vampires, or *empusas* of Greece, who were able to take on the appearance of beautiful women. They were always trying to get handsome young men to fall in love with them, and marry them. When they were successful, they would drink the blood of the poor bridegrooms. That's a rather nasty wedding present.

The ancient Greeks also had the *lamias,* who seemed to have three talents. They could remove their own eyes. They could turn into beautiful women. And they could drink a tremendous amount of blood. These creatures were said to have existed in central Africa.

Then there were the *striges,* who were also found in ancient Greece. They seemed to prefer the blood of young children. Instead of changing into beautiful women, the striges changed into birds. Some stories say they flew into the nurseries and drank the blood of the sleeping children.

In France, during the fifth and sixth centuries, some laws were passed concerning vampires. One of them said, "If any one shall testify that another has acted as héréburge or strioporte — titles applied to those who carry the copper vessel to the spot where the vampires perform their enchantments — and if he fail to convict him, he shall be condemned thereby to a forfeit of 7,500 deniers, being 180½ sous . . . If a vampire shall devour a man and be found guilty, she shall forfeit 8,000 deniers, being 200 sous."

Originally, however, the modern vampire was a Slavonic creature, sticking pretty closely to the countries of Hungary, Czechoslovakia, Romania, and the Balkan States. His legend seems to have started just before the beginning of the sixteenth century. And by the seventeenth century, the belief in these ghosts began to spread further west.

A book was written by Allaci, a Greek writer, and published in Cologne, Germany, in 1645. It was partly responsible for spreading the vampire legend into Europe. Also by this time, travelers from the western part of Europe began to hear strange tales on their journeys through eastern Europe. When they returned home, they spread these stories around to thrill their friends and neighbors.

The belief in vampires was strengthened in 1706, when a short book on them appeared in Czechoslovakia. One of the chapters told of a woman who had died and was buried. About four days later, a monster was seen in the village. It kept reappearing, sometimes in the shape of a dog, sometimes in the shape of a man. But it was always roaming around, choking people and killing cattle. The body of the woman was uncovered and

I. N. J.
DISSERTATIO
HISTORICO-PHILOSOPHICA
De
MASTICATIONE
MORTUORUM,
Quam
Dei & Superiorum indultu,
in illuftri Academ. Lipf.
fiftent
PRÆSES
M. PHILIPPUS Rohr / Marckran-
ftadio-Mifnic.
&
RESPONDENS
BENJAMIN FRIZSCHIUS, Mufilaviâ-Mifnicus,
Alumni Electorales.
ad diem XVI. Augufti Ann. M. DC. LXXIX.
H. L. Q. C.

LIPSIÆ,
Typis MICHAELIS VOGTII.

DE MASTICATIONE MORTUORUM
By Philip Rohr

The poster announces a lecture on how to feed the dead. The lecture was presented by Philip Rohr at the University of Leipzig in 1679.

burned. Oddly enough the chokings and killings stopped.

Of course, that was a story of a rather amateurish vampire who probably did not know how to get a square meal. But in 1746, a French monk, published a big book on vampires and ghosts. It told how vampires were really supposed to act. And it wasn't long before the bloodthirsty creatures were feared and discussed in most of Europe.

More and more stories kept appearing. In the early eighteenth century, some strange practices were reported on the Greek island of St. Erini (Santorini). The people there thought that they were being tormented by vampires. They began to dig up bodies from graveyards all over the island and promptly burned the corpses. As people on the island would die, their relatives would cut the feet, hands, noses, and ears from the bodies (a practice called acroteriazein) and tie these parts to the elbows of the corpse. Supposedly the maimed body would not be able to rise from the grave to haunt the living.

Some of the people who kept the vampire legend going, of course, were the fiction writers. Vampires appeared in poems by Goethe, Lord Byron, and Southey. One of the most popular plays in Paris of the 1820's was about a vampire. A German vampire opera was written in 1828, and Alexandre Dumas wrote a vampire play in the 1850's.

A book reprinted in 1853, called *Varney the Vampire*, caused the biggest sensation! Originally written by Thomas Preskett Prest, it was an 868 page monster. But when a publisher named E. Lloyd brought it out in penny parts, it really caught on. Then came *Dracula*,

Bram Stoker's classic vampire novel, published in 1897. And this was the beginning of the vampire as a commercial enterprise. The legends are still copied in stories and movies even today.

Recently, historians have come to believe that Stoker patterned his horrible account after two real characters. One of them was a Romanian nobleman and the other was a Hungarian countess.

Vlad IV was a fifteenth century ruler from the province of Wallachia, which later became a part of the country of Romania. He was the son of a rather cruel ruler, too. His father was referred to as Vlad the Devil, and the word devil was translated into *Dracul*. Vlad IV soon earned himself an appropriate nickname, in addition to *Draculaea* (Son of the Devil). The peasants began calling him Vlad the Impaler, because of one of his more unpleasant hobbies.

Vlad had one ambition — to keep control of his little kingdom by preventing uprisings by the peasants and invasions by the Turks. After one victory, he ordered the whole group of prisoners to be impaled on sharp stakes. The officers were to have the highest stakes, however, because of their superior rank. In another battle, it is said that he killed more than ten thousand Turks.

No. 1.] Nos. 2, 3 and 4 are Presented, Gratis, with this No. [Price 1d.

VARNEY THE VAMPIRE.
OR THE
FEAST OF BLOOD

A ROMANCE OF EXCITING INTEREST.

BY THE AUTHOR OF
" GRACE RIVERS; OR, THE MERCHANT'S DAUGHTER."

LONDON: E. LLOYD, SALISBURY-SQUARE, AND ALL BOOKSELLERS.

Here's Varney!
The frontispiece
from the 1847
novel, *Varney
the Vampire.*

After taking care of the Turkish troops for a while, he turned on the Saxons, who were invading from the west. When he captured a town called Brasov, he was not satisfied with killing soldiers, he persecuted the civilians as well. Forty-one local merchants were impaled there, and three hundred peasants were burned at the stake. This last group, of course, included many women and children.

It is said that he sometimes ordered an entire village population to be impaled. After one battle, at least, he wandered among the wounded of his own army, investigating their injuries. If they were wounded in the front of their bodies, they were given medals. But if, however, their wounds were in the back, Vlad assumed that they had been running away from the battle, and had them impaled.

Vlad was finally defeated and sentenced to twelve years in prison in a fortress on the Danube River. After his prison term had expired, he was put under house arrest in the city of Pest (now part of Budapest). While he was there, an army officer entered the house in a manner that did not suit Vlad (he probably forgot to bow low enough), and so Vlad had the poor man's head cut off.

For some reason, the people restored this evil man to the throne of Wallachia in 1476. There are those who never learn. At any rate, he came to the end of his days in a battle with the Turks, and his head was sent back to Istanbul.

But the story was not over even then. Vlad's body — minus its head — was buried in the church of Snagov Monastery. Many years later, the grave was opened, and the only things that were to be found in it were a broken urn and the moldering bones of a horse. Draw your own conclusions.

Now on to Countess Elizabeth Bathory, who was born in the late sixteenth century. It is possible that this little lady also played an important part in the development of the Dracula story. She murdered over six hundred young women in her Castle Csejthe in Hungary. And it is said that she did this for the sheer pleasure of taking a bath in their blood.

She traveled in her black coach all over the countryside looking for girls — always at night. When a girl was found, she was kidnaped and imprisoned in the castle. She was tied up, and the countess had her blood slowly drained from her body. Some of the blood she drank, the rest of it she bathed in.

Finally, word of these strange happenings reached the ears of King Matthias II of Hungary. He had the castle stormed and a number of girls were found in the dungeon, hanging, pale and bloodless from their chains.

The dreaded
Countess Elizabeth Bathory.

So Elizabeth was tried and convicted, and sentenced to be walled up alive. It is said that even today her screams can be heard coming from that walled-up room in Castle Csejthe.

What is a vampire supposed to look like? Well, he is usually thin, but he may look like a long-dead corpse. He could be dressed in the clothing in which he was buried, or he might dress like anyone else that you would meet in the street (or in an old haunted castle).

At times he may run to fat, being gorged with blood. His lips are thick and very red. When he smiles, you will notice that his canine teeth are long and sharp. In some parts of Russia, it is believed that the vampire's teeth are made of steel. And often the creature's hands are numb because they have remained crossed in the grave for so long. So some say he usually gnaws his way out of his coffin with his horrible, metallic fangs.

His skin is white with the color of death, and he is usually icy cold to the touch. When attacking a victim, he is supposed to have gleaming eyes that may give off a red light from time to time. His hands are hairy, and the hair extends to the palms. His eyebrows meet over the nose, with pointed, claw-like fingernails, and pointed ears, not an especially appealing dinner companion. His strength is enormous. And one more thing, he has bad breath.

One of the best descriptions of these beasts was written by a German school director in the mid-eighteenth century:

"The *Vampyres,* which come out of the Graves in the Night-time, rush upon People sleeping in their Beds, suck out all their Blood, and destroy them. They attack Men, Women, and Children, sparing neither Age nor Sex. The People attacked by them complain of Suffocation, and a great Interception of Spirits;

after which, they soon expire. Some of them, being asked, at the Point of Death, what is the Matter with them, say they suffer in the Manner just related from people lately dead, or rather the Spectres of those People; upon which, their Bodies, from the Description given of them, by the sick Person, being dug out of the Graves, appear in all Parts, as the Nostrils, Cheeks, Breast, Mouth. &c. turgid and full of Blood. Their Countenances are fresh and ruddy; and their Nails, as well as Hair, very much grown. And though they have been much longer dead than many other Bodies, which are perfectly putrified, not the least Mark of Corruption is visible upon them. Those who are destroyed by them, after their Death, become *Vampyres;* so that, to prevent so spreading an Evil, it is found requisite to drive a stake through the dead Body, from whence, on this Occasion, the Blood flows as if the Person was alive. Sometimes the Body is dug out of the Grave, and burnt to Ashes; upon which, all Disturbances cease."

That tells you something about the classic vampire. But there are amusing little exceptions to the description. Some Bulgarians believed that a true vampire had only one nostril. And there were a few Polish people who thought that his tongue was either pointed or had a barb on the end. Greek vampires are sometimes described as having blue eyes. But that may have been just an example of a disguise for self-protection.

At one time or another, people have been accused of being vampires just because they may have had red hair or a harelip. Perhaps they had strange birthmarks. Or they may have been born with their teeth already growing through their gums.

So much for the physical characteristics of the vampire. It is said that this creature can live on and on forever, if he is not killed in the proper way. And he cannot throw a shadow. As the hero of *Dracula*, Jonathan Harker, said when he was approached by some female vampire beauties: ". . . though the moonlight was behind them, they threw no shadow on the floor."

Of course, if they don't cast shadows, you would also expect that they would not be reflected in the mirror. Again the hero of Dracula: "There could be no error, for the man was close to me, and I could see him over my shoulder. But there was no reflection of him in the mirror! The whole room behind me was displayed; but there was no sign of a man in it, except myself."

Vampires reportedly have the ability to change themselves into animals, or dust, or a mist. They can also make themselves small. In fact, they have many mysterious and remarkable characteristics. Let's talk about a few more.

An old painting,
"The Resuscitated Corpse,"
comes from the Wiertz Museum.

TWO / THE HOME LIFE OF THE UNDEAD /

The Vampire stories always seem to take place close to the vampire's own grave. Some believe that he needs to get back into his tomb or coffin before daylight so that he can sleep all day. Other stories say that he must get to shelter before the first cock crows. The reason may be due to an ancient Greek belief that the rooster has magical properties. Supposedly his crow at dawn frightens away evil spirits.

But you can't feel too safe even in the daylight. Some stories are told of happy vampires wandering around in the warm sun.

Keep in mind that not all vampires are troublemakers, however. There is a legend on the Greek island of Santorini about a cobbler named Alexander. After he died, he turned into a vampire, but all that he did was to come back to his home and help out his widow. He mended his children's shoes, fetched water for his wife, cut wood

for the fire, and, in general, made himself useful around the house.

But the usual kind of vampire gets up from his grave when night comes again. If you consider that some of these creatures are able to open a coffin lid and climb out through six feet of soil, you should come to the conclusion that our average vampire must have magical powers. Perhaps he comes out of the grave as a mist or as some sort of animal.

Let's take a look at the kinds of animals that he most often changes into. The legends talk of cats, wolves, or owls. There are only a few tales about a vampire turning himself into a bat. This idea is almost pure Hollywood. We say almost however, because perhaps the bat idea may have come from travelers who went to South America during the nineteenth century. They came back with stories of a strange beast—the vampire bat which reportedly sucked the blood of cattle.

These illustrations from
the nineteenth century show what some people
thought vampire bats looked like.

The American
Indians also had
their bat-people.

There was really no reason for humans to fear these
South American bats, however. The creatures do not
even suck blood. They merely bite the victim and lick
up the blood as it flows out of the wound. Besides, the
bats are so small that about the only thing they could
kill would be a mouse or a small bird.

Of course, if a human being were to permit himself to
be bitten over and over again, he might wind up with a
shortage of blood, but who would be that silly? Unfortunately, though, there is the danger of getting rabies or
some other disease from these flying mammals. So it is
better to stay away from them.

And there are places where people believe in the magical powers of the bat. The Far East is one of these areas.
In the Tyrol, a section of the Alps between Austria and
Italy, if you want to become invisible, it is said that you
must wear the left eye of a bat. Or if you live in the town
of Hesse, in Germany, just tie the heart of a bat to your

arm with red thread, and you will encounter some good fortune.

But these superstitions have nothing to do with vampires. And the bat seems to have little connection with the vampire, except in horror movies.

So our next question is, what does the vampire do when he finds a likely-looking victim? Again, Jonathan Harker, the hero of *Dracula,* explains after finding his wife lying unconscious.

"Just over the external jugular vein there were two punctures, not large, but not wholesome-looking. There was no sign of disease, but the edges were white and worn-looking, as if by some trituration [grinding]."

But the poor man soon found out by personal experience what his wife had gone through.

"Then the skin of my throat began to tingle as one's flesh does when the hand that is to tickle it approaches nearer—nearer. I could feel the soft, shivering touch of the lips on the super-sensitive skin of my throat, and the hard dents of two sharp teeth, just touching and pausing there. I closed my eyes . . . and waited— waited with beating heart."

How do these vampires get away with their tricks? Some experts say that a vampire hypnotizes his victims.

How else can he get the poor unfortunate to hold still? Later, the bitten individual will wake up feeling a little tired, but he will probably remember nothing about his experience.

Some Russians believe in a few unusual types of vampires. One of them seems to work by remote control. He stays in his grave all the time, chewing on his own hands and feet. And as he does this, his relatives, one by one, sicken and die. Another Russian vampire has rather bad aim. He does not bite the neck of his victim, but chews on his chest. One kind of Russian vampire does not bite at all. He sneaks up on a sleeping person and hits him in the back. Immediately the back opens up and blood comes running out. The vampire merely fills a convenient bucket with the blood and drinks it.

According to various myths, there are several different ways to become a vampire. The usual way is, of course, to be bitten by one and have him drink your blood. But other people believe that anyone dying in a state of sin will become a vampire. Actually, there are a variety of ways; dying after being cursed by one's parents, committing suicide, lying in court, or being excommunicated from the church. There are people in parts of Mexico and Burma who profess that a woman who dies in childbirth automatically becomes a vampire. And if her child dies with her, it will become a vampire too.

Romania was full of vampire legends. One superstition said unbaptized people became vampires when they died. Or if a woman was seen by a vampire while she was pregnant and did not receive a priest's blessing, her child would become this horrible creature. But that is not all. Some thought that werewolves became vampires after they died. (That's really stretching the imagination.)

Another myth from Greece said that if you were born in Greece on Christmas Day or even any time between Christmas and Epiphany, you might become a vampire. Or if you were the seventh son or the seventh daughter born to your parents, look out.

One of the weirdest superstitions comes from the Balkans. In Bulgaria and Serbia (Yugoslavia) it is thought that if a bird flies over a corpse, or a cat or a dog jumps over a body, the dead person will become a vampire. And it will be a particularly nasty one, too. Not only will it drink the blood of its victims, but it will also rip out their hearts to roast over a slow fire.

There is a cure for this. Place a piece of iron in the hand of the corpse before it is buried.

There were various ways to get rid of unwanted horrors. Garlic and hawthorn have been known for centuries to frighten off vampires. The Greeks and Turks used to believe that eating garlic was a protection from vampires. It probably kept everybody else away, also.

Gustave Doré used
frightening bat-people to
populate Hell, in this illustration
from Dante's *Inferno*.

The Mohammedan tradition says that this plant sprang up from the left footprint of Satan as he was being thrown out of heaven. (The onion appeared in his right footprint.) All over the world people have been known to use garlic to ward off evil spirits.

Sometimes this vegetable was hung over the doors of houses and the sterns of boats to guard people from ghosts.

The characters in *Dracula* were big on garlic, but they used another substance, too. It was the concentrated wafer from a church communion service. This scene (from *Dracula*) is outside the tomb of a vampire. Harker describes:

"First he [a doctor who is a vampire expert] took from his bag a mass of what looked like a thin, wafer-like biscuit, which was carefully rolled up in a white napkin; next he took out a double-handful of some whitish stuff, like dough or putty. He crumbled the

wafer up fine and worked it into the mass between his hands. This he then took, and rolling it into thin strips, began to lay them into the crevices between the door and its setting in the tomb. . .

" 'I am closing the tomb, so that the Un-dead may not enter.'

" 'And is that stuff you have put there going to do it?'. . .

" 'What is that which you are using?'. . .

" 'The Host.' "

Anyone who has ever seen a vampire film knows that these ghosts are afraid of a crucifix. And if the crucifix is made of silver, so much the better, since vampires are afraid of that metal. A freshly-buried coffin may contain a vampire, but iron skewers thrust straight down into the earth that covers the grave could prevent the dead body from arising.

A suspected vampire can also be buried under running water. Supposedly he will not be able to cross a moving stream or river. But don't always count on this, however; there are several stories about a vampire who was able to rent a boat.

There is an old superstition in Serbia that vampires cannot pass through a door marked with a cross painted in tar. On the Isle of Man, which lies between Ireland and England, some people hang mayflower or rowan (a tree

Two clay figures and a sheep's heart pierced with hawthorn twigs are nailed to a castle door. Hawthorn was thought to have magical powers.

related to the mountain ash) over their door. A sprig of hawthorn can come in handy also. When approached by a vampire, just throw the hawthorn on the ground. The vampire will be so busy picking it up, you can run away from him (or so some say).

There were other people who must have thought that vampires were not very bright either. One old method of getting rid of them was to throw mustard seeds around the house, or at the doorway, or even on the roof. The idea was that the vampire would have to count every seed that he found, and so he would not have time to chase you.

If everything else fails, you can repeat this ancient Chaldean spell:

"Talisman, talisman, boundary that cannot be taken away, boundary that the gods cannot pass, barrier immovable, which is opposed to malevolence! whither it be a wicked Utuq, a wicked Alal, a wicked Gigim, a wicked god, a wicked Maskim, a phantom, a spectre, a vampire, an incubus, a succubus, a nightmare, may the barrier of the god Ea stop him!"

Suppose that a vampire is loose in the neighborhood, How is he found? One way is to look at graves. When finger holes are found in the dirt covering the grave, this is a sign that there is a vampire buried there. These holes are the openings through which the vampire comes out of his grave (if he's thin enough).

Or the vampire's home can be found by using horses. First find a white stallion that has never stumbled. Then take him into the graveyard. Such a horse will refuse to walk on the grave of a vampire. In Serbia there is a belief that the vampire's grave is found by first placing a small boy on a coal black stallion. Then turn the horse loose in the graveyard. When the horse stops at a grave, it is sure to contain the body of a vampire.

If these methods do not work, the next step is to open all of the graves. In parts of Greece vampires cannot travel about on Fridays, so that would be the ideal day to look for them in their graves. If a body has not decomposed, and has red lips, long teeth, and blood smears on the face and hands, there is the culprit.

When the body of Count Dracula was finally found, Harker tells what he looked like:

> "There lay the Count, but looking as if his youth had been half renewed, for the white hair and moustache were changed to dark iron-gray; the cheeks were fuller, and the white skin seemed ruby-red underneath; the mouth was redder than ever, for on the lips were gouts of fresh blood, which trickled from the corners of the mouth and ran over the chin and neck. Even the deep, burning eyes seemed set amongst swollen flesh, for the lids and pouches underneath were bloated. It seemed as if the whole awful creature was simply gorged with blood. He lay like a filthy leech, exhausted with his repletion."

But once the vampire is found, what is done with him? Well, someone can shoot him with a silver bullet that has been blessed by a priest or a stake can be driven through his heart. There are some who say that only a white thorn stake will stop a vampire. And some Russians use the aspen stake. The traditional belief is that the stake must be driven in with one blow.

The stake treatment was the one used in *Dracula:* remember that they had found the vampire. . .

"Arthur placed the point [of the stake] over the heart. . . Then he struck with all his might.

"The Thing in the coffin writhed; and a hideous, bloodcurdling screech came from the open red lips. The body shook and quivered and twisted in wild contortions; the sharp white teeth clamped together till the lips were cut. . ."

Perhaps this whole stake belief originated with the ancient art of necromancy, or foretelling the future by using corpses. This ceremony must be older than the ancient Romans, because there are tales of its practice handed down by the Egyptians. The rite is quite complicated and varies considerably.

For nine days, the magician and his assistants prepare themselves for the ordeal by surrounding themselves with the aura of death. They wear used graveclothes, recite the funeral service countless times, and eat strange food. The diet consists of dog's flesh, unleavened and unsalted bread, and grape juice. No woman is allowed to enter into the ceremonies. Actually, if the magician even sees a woman, the whole ceremony may be ruined.

The magician must remain still throughout the entire nine days, thinking about death and especially the corpse that he is about to uncover. Then, at midnight of the ninth day, he draws a circle around the grave and burns a mixture of henbane, hemlock, aloes, wood, saffron, opium, and mandrake.

Then the grave is opened and the coffin lid is taken off. The magician touches the corpse three times, saying: "By the virtue of the Holy Resurrection and the agonies of the damned, I conjure and command thee, spirit of the deceased, to answer my demands and obey these sacred ceremonies, on pain of everlasting torment. Berald, Balbin, Gab, Gabor, Arise, Arise, I charge and command thee."

After this, the corpse will answer any question that the magician asks. At the last part of the ceremony, the magician puts the corpse back to death. To insure that it can never again be used for sorcery — he drives a stake through its heart.

There have been times however, when driving a stake through the heart did not work. There was the case of the dead herdsman in Bohemia (Czechoslovakia). This vampire had been killing people in the village of Blow, near Kadam. Finally the townspeople dug up his body and drove a stake through its heart. But while they were doing this, a voice came from the body and thanked them for giving him a stick with which to drive off the savage dogs of the neighborhood.

The next night the corpse removed the stake and began to kill the townspeople again. So several brave lads dug up the body, hung it, and burned it. That ended the trouble.

Some methods go further. There are those who recommend that the corpse's head also be cut off with a gravedigger's spade. Or, perhaps merely breaking the neck of the body is sufficient. Many people tried a variety of ways.

There is a Bulgarian belief that if some food is placed in a bottle, a vampire will go in after it. He is at that time in the shape of some pieces of straw. Then the bottle is capped and thrown into a fire. On one Greek island, when the vampire is found, his body is carried past 40 churches and replaced in the ground. That's a lot more work than sticking a stake through his heart.

There are places in the world where the people who find a vampire merely want to prevent him from rising out of his grave again. So they cut the leg muscles of the body and stick pins into its calves and thighs. But perhaps the most gruesome method of destroying a vampire was practiced in old Russia and Poland. The villagers made a paste out of his body and ate it.

In the seventeenth century, the historian, Allaci, made a study of vampires on the Greek island of Clio. He believed that the people there would never answer the first time that their names were called, for fear of speaking to a vampire. They only spoke when their names were uttered a second time. Apparently a vampire never repeated anything he said. On this island, the way to get rid of one was to dig up his body and burn it after saying some prayer. But three other methods were highly recommended also:

Tear out the vampire's heart and let the body rot above ground.

Cut off the head of the body.

Drive a large nail through its temple.

In other parts of Greece, after a vampire dies, his body does not rot, but swells up to a large size. The only way to turn these ghosts back to inactive corpses is to have their sins absolved by a priest. Then the body quickly decomposes.

Now there is a problem. In modern Greece there are those who believe that anybody who has led a saintly life will not decay after death. So, is an undecayed body a saint or a vampire? The answer to this is that the holy person gives off a sweet smell and the vampire smells rancid. Greece is not the only country where vampires are said never to rot. This story comes from Turkey:

An excommunicated man was buried in unconsecrated ground. His ghost caused a lot of unrest around the countryside, and when his body was dug up, it was found to be in its original state, with the blood still flowing in its veins. So the people cut up the body and boiled the pieces in wine. But what was to be done with the pieces? While the matter was being discussed, the family of the dead man had a priest give absolution to the remains. Immediately the parts of the man's body were changed to ashes.

But remember, if you are killed by a vampire, there may still be a chance for you. In certain parts of Russia, one myth professes that people who have been killed by a vampire can be brought back to life if they work fast enough. First find the vampire. Then cut off the left skirt of his burial shroud. Take that piece of cloth back to the room where the dead person is lying and lock the door. Then put some live coals in a pot, throw in the cloth, and the burning material will give off a smoke that will bring the dead person to life. So you see, there's still hope for all of us.

THREE / VAMPIRES AROUND THE WORLD /

There seems to be no doubt that almost every country has vampire legends. The Russians have their *upir* or *upuir*, and the Bulgarians have the *vapir*. There is the *vilkolak* in Poland, and the *wurwolaka* in Albania. In Greece, he is called the *vrykolaka*, and in Ireland, the *dearg-dul*. *Pamgri* is the name for the Hungarian vampire, and the *katakhana* is found in Crete. In Polynesia they talk of the *tii*, while the *hantu penyardin* is the Malayan vampire. Now let's explore a few vampire legends.

When we consider the vampire stories that have come out of Great Britain, it seems that a different breed of ghost roamed these islands. Oh, they were vampires, all right, but they were considered to be more gentle in their prowlings. Or at least they weren't as bloodthirsty as their relatives across the English Channel.

Take, for example, the case of the unnamed man of Buckinghamshire. Early in the twelfth century, a certain man died and was nicely buried by his wife and family. But the very next night, his ghost walked into the wife's bedroom, woke her up, and started jumping on her. The following night he did the very same thing.

Apparently the wife got tired of this (and who could blame her), because on the third night she invited her relatives in to sit up and wait for the ghost of her husband. When it appeared, all of the people began shouting and this frightened it away. But the vampire was not to be defeated so easily. He gave up trying to harm his wife and started picking on his brothers. But even they were able to chase him away.

Next, the vampire tried to harm the animals of the neighborhood. But the neighing and mooing kept the people of the village awake. Wearied by their loss of sleep, the townspeople asked their local priest for assistance. He wrote to the Bishop of Lincoln for help. The Bishop's first reaction was to consider uncovering the body and having it burned. But that seemed to be pretty drastic, since the vampire had not really hurt anyone.

So the Bishop decided on a more gentle solution. The body was raised (and the diggers were amazed to find that the corpse had not decayed a bit). Then a written notice of absolution was placed on the chest of the re-

Doctors used costumes such as this one to protect themselves during the plague. The snout of the costume was filled with spices which were thought to purify the air.

mains, the body was resealed in the coffin, and reburied. Wonder of wonders, the vampire was never seen again.

About the same time, in the twelfth century, there appeared a vampire in Berwick, Scotland. This was the ghost of a rich but wicked man. However, he just scared a lot of people by running up and down the streets at night. Apparently the smell he gave off upset the people more than his running around. Actually, they thought that this horrible odor would give them bubonic plague.

So ten brave men were given the job of digging up the body. They chopped it up into small pieces and threw it into a furnace. His ghost disappeared also.

There were Welch vampires, too. Here is the story of one, as written in the eleventh century by Walter Map, an English writer:

"I know of a strange portent that occurred in Wales. William Laudun or Landun, an English knight, strong of body and of proven valour, came to Gilbert Foliot, then Bishop of Hereford, now of London, and said: 'My Lord, I come to you for advise. A Welchman of evil life died of late unchristianly enough in my village, and straightaway after four nights took to coming back every night to the village, and will not desist from summoning singly and by name his fellow-villagers, who upon being called at once fall sick and die within three days, so that now there are very few of them left.'

"The Bishop, marvelling, said: 'Peradventure the Lord has given power to the evil angel of that lost soul to move about in the dead corpse. However, let the body be exhumed, cut the neck through with a spade, and sprinkle the body and the grave well with holy water, and replace it.'

"When this was done, the survivors were none the less plagued by the former illusion. So one night when the summoner had now left but few alive, he called William himself, citing him thrice. He, however, bold and quick as he was, and awake to the situation, darted out with his sword drawn, and chased the demon, who fled, up to the grave and there, as he fell into it, clave his head to the neck. From that hour the ravage of that wandering pestilence ceased, and did no more hurt either to William himself or to any one else."

Then there was the "Hundeprest," who also lived in the twelfth century. This nickname, meant "dog-priest," and it was given to a certain English chaplain who seemed to enjoy riding with the hounds in a fox hunt more than he did performing his churchly duties. When he died, his spirit returned to various bedrooms all over town.

This vampire was actually quite harmless. He stood and gurgled at his terrified victims, but fate caught up with him. One of the local priests brained him with an ax and the vampire ran back to his grave. When his body was uncovered, the ax wound could be seen on his head, and the coffin was filled with black blood. So they burned the body and scattered the ashes to the winds.

But not all British vampires were so innocent. During the very active twelfth century, in Yorkshire, there lived an extremely evil man who, nevertheless, seems to have been the victim of circumstances. He found out that his wife was being unfaithful to him, and he died shortly afterwards. He was buried in a Christian grave, but that didn't seem to prevent him from becoming a vampire.

It was said that often his ghost wandered around. Some believed that its sickening smell caused people to come down with the bubonic plague. The next Palm Sunday, a few of the people who had lost relatives in the plague decided to dig up the vampire's body. They found it covered by only a thin layer of earth. It was horribly swollen, with red puffed cheeks, and its burial wrappings were all torn and mutilated.

When one of the villagers bashed into the corpse with a spade, warm red blood began to flow all over. It was immediately supposed that this vampire had also been feeding off the blood of the townsfolk, so they burned the body. According to the story, the plague never again returned to the town.

About the same time, there lived an English knight who had recently been married. The marriage was ideal, except for a few incidents. The morning after the birth of their first child, the knight and his wife found that their baby boy had been murdered—his throat was cut from ear to ear.

The same thing happened after the birth of their second child. After the birth of their third child, the family sat up all night in the nursery, but the same thing happened.

Finally, at the birth of their fourth child, another boy, they invited the neighbors in for the night. Then they lighted lamps and torches all over their property, and waited, guarding the child.

During the night a stranger appeared. He claimed to have been on a long journey, and was welcomed into the castle. The newcomer volunteered to sit up with the group. And later, everyone except the stranger seemed to fall into a mysterious sleep. It was he alone who was able to see that one of the women who had been on guard went to the cradle and was about to cut the throat of the new-born boy.

The stranger shouted, everyone woke up and the men seized the woman. They took a key to the local church, heated it in a fire, and branded her on the forehead.

But the real surprise came when another woman, the exact double of the vampire, entered the room. It seems that the vampire had assumed the identity of this second woman. At that point, the hostage shrieked and flew out of the window, disappearing forever.

Then a strange thing happened in Britain. After the twelfth century, stories about vampires seemed to die out. Except for a few very rare exceptions, no mention is made of this type of ghost until the nineteenth century.

Probably the first reason that caused its return was Thomas Preskett Prest's book, *Varney the Vampire* (or *The Feast of Blood*). Prest followed this with many other shockers. There was *The Goblet of Gore, The Death Grasp, The Maniac Father,* and many more. Then *Dracula* appeared and the vampire in England was once more an established ghost.

In the late nineteenth century, along came the supposedly true report of Croglin Grange. This was an old house in Cumberland, owned by a family named Fisher. The Fisher family grew and grew, and they felt that they ought to move to a bigger house. So they rented Croglin Grange to two brothers and a sister.

The trouble began one hot summer night. The sister had gone to bed and lay watching the scenery through her window. Suddenly she noticed two lights flickering in a nearby wood. The lights grew closer and closer, and when the sister jumped out of bed to run to the door to get help, she was terrified by a kind of scratching noise at her window.

She turned to the window, and beheld a hideous brown face with flaming eyes glaring in at her. She rushed back to her bed for some reason or other, only to find that the beast had now broken in the window pane and was advancing across the bedroom toward her. The girl was so frightened that she could not scream. The creature came up to the bed, twisted its long bony fingers through her hair, dragged her head to the side of the bed, and bit her violently on the neck.

As she was being bitten, her voice apparently came back to her, and she screamed. Her brothers heard her and broke through the door. They found that the beast had escaped through the window while their sister lay on her bed in a faint.

She did recover, and, naturally enough, all three of them decided to take a vacation away from this house of horror. They went to Switzerland for a long holiday and, strangely, when autumn was approaching, it was the sister who suggested that they return to the house in England.

The following March, the sister was awakened again by the scratching of her old acquaintance. But this time she could scream, and her brothers were able to give chase to the creature, shooting it in the leg. But the ghost escaped. He ran right into an old burial vault.

The next day the brothers gathered all of their neighbors and went to search the vault. They were horrified to find that the coffins in the vault had been opened and all of the bodies had been mutilated and their parts had been scattered around. Only one coffin was undisturbed. They opened that one and found the horrible creature that had attacked the sister. When they saw the fresh

This seventeenth century print
shows one of the earliest examples
of raising the dead—the Witch of Endor
calling up the biblical prophet Samuel.

gunshot wound in its leg, they realized that there was only one thing to do with the body. So they burned it.

Vampire legends are not unknown in Ireland, either. A tale is told about a priest who died in the early twentieth century. His funeral service was completed, and he was to be buried in a plot some distance away. The priest's grieving mother was too upset to make the journey to the cemetery, and stayed home. When the burial had been completed, the mourners came back to the mother's house.

When they got there, they found the old woman lying face down on the floor of her living room. After they picked her up and laid her on the bed, it took them quite a long time to bring her back to consciousness. Then she told them the horrible story.

Schwillinger fecit

Viro Nobilissimo, Excellentissimo, Domino DAVDE THOMAN, JC.to Consiliario Rein. Au-
gustanæ Primario, Scholarchæ meritiss. &c. Artium Fautori, Æstimatoriq. magno
æquivi cultus gratia offert, et dicat Johann Heinrich Schönfeld

It seems that she had heard footsteps on the front walk, and then she heard a knock at the door. When she opened the door, she saw her dead son standing there. His eyes were blazing, his skin was deathly white, and his teeth were much longer than they had been when he was alive. When she saw this vampire, the mother fainted, and the vampire disappeared, never to be seen again.

There have been tales of vampires in the United States. Most of these are just as questionable and not as exciting. Many are accounts of how dead bodies were thought to be feeding on the life juices of their close relatives and thereby making them ill. The bodies were usually taken out of their graves and burned.

From France there comes the story of the vampire trial of a certain Sergeant Bertrand. This court proceeding started on July 10, 1849, and attracted a large crowd.

The tale went this way. For months, cemeteries in and around Paris had been vandalized. Some of the guards at the cemeteries claimed that they had seen ghostly figures flitting around the graves. When morning came, many graves were found opened and bodies mutilated. Sometimes this happened after a person had just been buried.

Finally, the guards at one of the cemeteries were able to get close enough to one of the creatures to shoot him, but he escaped. However, some scraps of a military uniform were discovered at the scene. That night a Sergeant Bertrand checked into a military hospital, suffering from gunshot wounds. He confessed to these grave-robbing crimes, and was sentenced to one year in prison.

Another French tale dates from the early eighteenth century. There was a man, Viscount de Morière, who had a very strange appearance. He was tall and thin, with a pointed forehead and protruding teeth. Supposedly he had a bad habit of cutting off the heads of all of his servants—one person at a time. The people around the countryside became very alarmed and they killed the Viscount.

After he was buried, an epidemic of deaths began—all of the victims were children and all of them died with vampire toothmarks on their throats. For a time the killings would stop, and then they would begin all over again. After 72 years passed, the grandson of the Viscount inherited his title.

The young Viscount had heard of his grandfather's problem, and now, for the first time, it was within his power to open the grave of the old man and hold an investigation. When the lid of the coffin was removed, the body of the dead man was found to be undecayed. His face was flushed and there was blood in his heart and chest. His skin was soft and natural.

As the story is told, a white thorn was driven through its head. The corpse began to scream and blood and water flowed out of the wound. Then the body was burned. No more suspicious deaths occurred.

Hungary is one of the countries where the vampire legend is the strongest. Not only that, but some believe that the Hungarian vampires are among the ugliest and most gruesome.

One of these myths is about a shoemaker in Silesia who, in 1591, cut his own throat with a knife. His family was shocked and tried to hide what really happened by saying that he had died in a fit. After the funeral and the burial, the townsfolk were soon bothered by a vampire who would jump on them in the dark of night.

As time went on, the vampire became even more troublesome, appearing in the daytime, too. The trouble continued for about eight months. Finally, the natives asked the mayor of the town if they could uncover the shoemaker's body.

When the body was taken from the coffin, it appeared to be freshly dead—no decay, no smell. The only difference between the body and the living man was a little mark in the shape of a rose on his right big toe. The people thought it would be a good idea to rebury the body under a gallows, but even that did not work. The prowling continued.

After a month of this, the body was uncovered again. This time it appeared to be a little fatter than before. So they cut off its head, arms, and legs, and opened up the corpse so that the heart could be removed. Then they burned all of the pieces, put them into a sack, and threw the sack into the river.

The treatment worked—the vampire was never seen again. But his memory lingered on. When one of the shoemaker's maids died later, it turned out that she had become a vampire also and attacked babies in their cribs. This time the townspeople knew just what to do. They dug her up and did the same thing that they had done to the shoemaker's body.

Probably one of the most troublesome vampires of all times was Johannes Cuntius, who died in Silesia in the sixteenth century. He had been kicked by a horse, and at the moment of his death, all of the animals of the neighborhood were suddenly restless and noisy. No one could understand why. Even Cuntius' cat leaped on the corpse's face and scratched it.

During the next eight months, the reports say that Johannes the Vampire drove everyone nearly crazy. He would enter houses at night, terrify the inhabitants, and throw their possessions around. It is said that he even tried to drink the blood of his widow's housemaid, and that he killed a child.

Sometimes ghosts
do not take kindly
to being raised
from the grave.

Next, the vampire started to pick on just one man in the village. First he entered this poor man's bedroom to attack him. But he was driven off. (No one seems to know how.) Then the vampire caused the lips of the man's son to grow together so that he could not open his mouth. He tried, unsuccessfully, to kidnap one of the maids in the house, and he assumed the shape of a dwarf to attack the man's wife. Finally, he took on the shape of a pig to attack the man's cook.

Because of the unusual circumstances of Cuntius's death, the townspeople decided to investigate his grave. When they arrived at the cemetery, they found that the gravestone had been overturned and that many holes around the area were actually tunnels leading to the coffin. Inside the grave they found the body in perfect condition. When they tried to drive a stake into him, the vampire knocked it out of their hands. (He must have been pretty strong.)

So they decided to burn him. But when they tried to lift the body out of the coffin with ropes, he suddenly became so heavy that the ropes broke. Finally it took the efforts of a large horse to raise the body from the ground, and he was cut up and burned. Mr. Cuntius, or Mr. Cuntius's vampire, never bothered the townspeople again.

In 1720, some strange stories were heard in the Hungarian town of Haidam — a place that seems to have had some very special kinds of vampires. It was said that on several occasions a family of the town would be sitting down to dinner when they would be joined by a stranger. At the end of the meal, the stranger, apparently still hungry, would jump on one of the members of the family and bite his or her neck. This unusually greedy vampire was killed by driving a twopenny nail right through his temples.

There is also a Hungarian story of a vampire named Grando, who seemed to be sorry that he was one. When some men opened his grave, he appeared to be happy that they had found his body, for he smiled at them. A priest was brought to the body and, holding up a crucifix, he said: "Raise thine eyes and look upon Jesus Christ who hath redeemed us from the pains of hell by His Most Holy Passion and His Precious Death upon the rood."

Grando's face lit up and tears of joy began to run down his cheeks. Then the men cut off his head.

The belief in vampires did not die in Hungary. In 1909, a Vienna newspaper reported that a castle in the Carpathian mountains had been burned by the people in a nearby town. There had been an epidemic of child deaths in the community, and the natives blamed it on a vampire—the ghost of a count who had owned the castle years before. It's difficult to say whether the act of arson helped at all.

And as recently as 1912, a Budapest newspaper ran a story about a farmer who claimed that he had been attacked by the vampire of a 14 year old boy. The farmer and a few friends went to the graveyard and dug up the body of the boy. They put three pieces of garlic and three stones into his mouth, and then drove a stake through his chest. Supposedly the vampire disappeared.

Finally, one of the most recent stories concerns Fritz Haarman, the Hanover (Germany) vampire. On April 17, 1925, Londoners were startled when they read the following item in the *Daily Express:*

VAMPIRE BRAIN. PLAN TO PRESERVE IT FOR SCIENCE *Berlin. Thursday, April 16th.* The body of Fritz Haarman, executed yesterday at Hanover for twenty-seven murders, will not be buried until it has been examined at Gottingen University.

Owing to the exceptional character of the crimes — most of Haarman's victims were bitten to death — the case aroused tremendous interest among German scientists. It is probable that Haarman's brain will be removed and preserved by the University authorities. — Central News.

Haarman was born in Hanover in 1879. When he was a young man, he joined the army and was to have been a pretty good soldier. But after his discharge, he was accused many times of harming children. Finally, he was committed to a mental hospital. He managed to escape from the institution and rejoined the army. (Why the military took him is unexplained.) When he was discharged again, he returned to Hanover and took up the professions of thievery, burglary, and occasionally, fraud.

But they caught him. And, after a long prison term, he returned home in 1918 and opened a combination meat market and restaurant. Surprisingly, the meat market was a great success with the housewives of the neighborhood. Probably because Fritz was able to sell meat at lower prices than the other butchers of Hanover. But in the end the local ladies inevitably regretted their purchases. Haarman was tried and convicted of killing between twenty-four and fifty young boys.

Worst of all, it was said that he had killed them by biting their throats and then eating them. Some think he sold the flesh that he himself couldn't eat.

Unfortunately, no report of any exciting findings came from the study of Haarman's brain. And the German doctors and scientists learned nothing new about vampires.

Like the vampires themselves, stories of vampirism do not die easily. Some of these creatures were merely murderers who had extraordinarily bloodthirsty methods of killing. Many were probably the results of over-exaggerating or fear. But who can say that all of them were imaginary figures of hysterical people?

OTHER GHOSTS

FOUR / THE ZOMBIE AND SOME OF HIS FRIENDS / An amazing law was passed by the

New York City Council in 1962. The men of this dignified group passed a law forbidding the sale of Voodoo drugs in the city. The list prevented the sale of bat's blood, grave dust, lover's oil, and candles with prayers written on them, such as "Death unto my enemy."

This law is just one of many examples that illustrates how little most people know about the practice of Voodoo. Ask almost any man in the street about this religion, and he will probably tell you that it is a primitive form of magic. He may even suggest that its followers believe in ghosts. What the majority of people seem to know about Voodoo probably comes from the horror films that they have seen in theaters and on television. Here, Voodoo appears not to be much more than witchdoctors sticking pins in dolls and creating zombies (people who rise from the dead).

But the truth is that Voodoo is a very complex religion. And its followers are just as intense about their beliefs as are Christians, Jews, Buddhists, or Moslems. There is reason to believe that the rituals and symbols of Voodoo are as old or older than those of almost any of our modern faiths. They go back thousands of years.

It would seem that Voodoo came to the Western World about two hundred years ago. It was at that time that the slave raids began on the West Coast of Africa. The African natives were captured and taken to the West Indies and sold to plantation owners.

But they brought with them their own religion, which was based upon the worship of the god, Vodu. Gradually, Vodu became more than a god. He became the symbol of the sect, the ceremonies, the priests and priestesses, and all of the people who believed in him. So we find that the religion came to be called *Vodu, Voodoo, Voudou, Vaudau, Voudoux,* or *Vaudaux.* And, in recent times, it has been referred to as *Hoodoo* by some people.

The religion spread quickly, and the slave owners feared it. As early as 1782, the governor of Louisiana stopped the importation of slaves from Martinique, an island in the West Indies, because they practiced Voodoo. He said that these slaves "would make the lives of the citizens unsafe." In 1792, Louisiana likewise banned slaves who had come from Haiti—for the same reason.

Soon many of the slave owners in the Western Hemisphere were terrified of the religious beliefs of the same people whom they were treating so cruelly. The anthropologist, Alfred Métraux, described it this way: ". . . the fear which reigned in the plantations had its source in the deeper recesses of the soul: it was the witchcraft of remote and mysterious Africa which troubled the sleep of the people in the 'big house.'"

The fear of Voodoo was not eased any by the publication of a book, *Hayti or the Black Republic.*

This book was written in 1884 by Spencer St. John, who was a British consul in Haiti at the time. He told stories of cannibalism, child sacrifice, blood-baths, and murders. Most of it was untrue or highly exaggerated but it was this book that appears to be the basic text for all of the scary movies and sensational newspaper stories which have been devoted to Voodoo ever since.

As a matter of fact, most people consider that Haiti is the hotbed of the Voodoo religion. This is not exactly true. Voodoo exists in many parts of the world. It can be found in Africa in its old forms. In South America it exists under the names of Macumba and Candomblé. And it has spread itself to the United States, too. In 1959, a principal of an elementary school in Wetumka, Alabama, was forced to resign because she was charged with teaching Voodooism. In 1962, the year that Voodoo

The plan of a
seventeenth century slave ship,
showed slaves packed in
like animals.

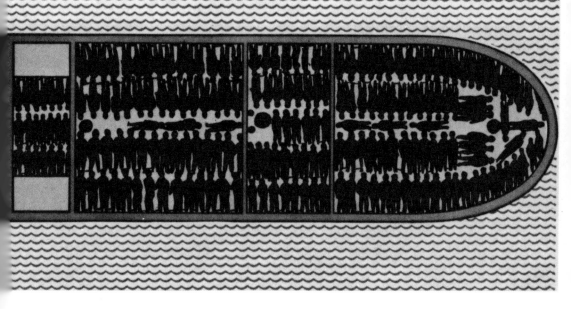

drugs were prohibited in New York City, a Phoenix, Arizona, woman shot her husband while, as she said, "under the spell of a Voodoo doctor." She was given a year's suspended sentence.

Voodoo is a complicated religion, as are most religions. There is not enough space in any book to go into all of its practices and beliefs. So the question we're concerned about in this book is — how does the believer in Voodoo regard the dead?

To begin, they believe that every person's body contains a soul. It is not the same kind of soul that you find in Christian teachings. It is formed by two spirits. Spirit number one is the *gros-bon-ange* (the big good angel). This represents the person's personality, experiences, and intelligence. Spirit number two is the *ti-bon-ange* (the good little angel). This represents the person's conscience.

After death, it is believed that the soul, with its two spirits, must spend at least one year at the bottom of a stream or river. Then the soul begins to grow impatient. It starts warning its friends or family that it wishes to leave its watery grave. Now the friends or family must decide whether or not to have a ceremony called *retirer d'en bas de l'eau* (drawing out from the bottom of the water). In this ritual, the soul of the dead person is called out and placed in a kind of jar called a *govi*.

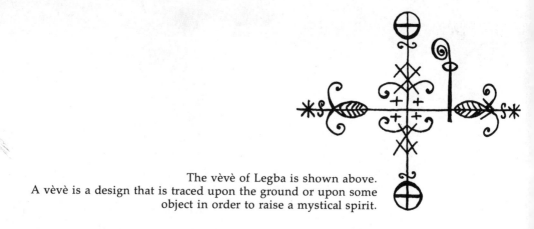

The vèvè of Legba is shown above.
A vèvè is a design that is traced upon the ground or upon some
object in order to raise a mystical spirit.

It is not surprising that some less attractive beliefs could have resulted from these practices.

The so-called *Black* Voodoo has become a favorite of non-believing writers over the years. A large part of this magical world concerns itself with black magic, sorcery, dreams, and zombies.

What is a zombie? W. B. Seabrook, an American writer, once described a zombie as "a soulless human corpse, still dead, but taken from the grave and endowed by sorcery with a mechanical semblance of life." And he went on to describe how people who really believed in zombies would guard the fresh grave of a relative until they were sure that the body had begun to rot away. They believed that a sorcerer cannot turn a rotten corpse into a zombie.

Seabrook claimed that he had seen zombies working in the Haitian canefields. He found them to be dull and plodding "with the eyes of a dead man, not blind, but staring, unfocused, unseeing."

The vèvè shown at the left
is of Baron Samedi,
the Voodoo god of the grave.

A native drawing
shows Baron Samedi.

The story is that a sorcerer makes zombies out of fresh corpses in order to provide cheap labor in the fields. Sometimes, it is said, they even hire out their dead slaves to farmers. But how do they create zombies in the first place?

The creation of a zombie by a sorcerer is done through the special help of the grand master of spells and sorceries. His name is *Legba-petro*, sometimes called *Maître Carrefour*. When the corpse is given life by one particular sorcerer, it becomes the slave of only that sorcerer.

It works like this. The sorcerer is supposed to hop on his horse and ride backwards to his victim's house. If the poor unfortunate is still alive, the sorcerer can kill him by sucking out his soul through a slit in the door. Then he blows the soul into a bottle that he has brought along for that purpose.

Shortly after this, the victim will die. After he is buried, the sorcerer will pray to Maître Carrefour, and then uncover the body. He holds the bottle containing the soul under the nose of the corpse, and the dead man will be animated as a zombie. There are some special drugs used at this point to aid in the magic. Although some people say that the process can be successful only if the corpse answers to its name.

It is also believed that the sorcerer does not have to kill his victim in order to turn him into a zombie. He may be able to "borrow" a body from a new grave. Apparently, all the sorcerer really needs is a fresh corpse.

There are ways to prevent a body from becoming a zombie. One is to guard the grave so the body can begin to decay. Another is to bury it under cement, or where people will always be around — by your doorway, for example, or at a crossroads. A corpse could be "killed" a second time by poisoning or strangling it. Or it could be buried with a dagger in its hand in order that it may protect itself from the sorcerer. Maybe the corpse's mouth would be sewn so that it could not answer its name when it was called.

However, there is one thing the sorcerer must always guard against if he wants to keep his zombies as slaves. It has been said that if a zombie accidentally eats meat or salt, he will snap out of his trance and remember that he is dead. Then he will go back to his grave and die again. And this time his death is permanent.

One of the most famous zombie stories is about a young society girl who died in Port-au-Prince, Haiti. A few years after her death, some of her friends said they saw her standing at a window in a house. The house was searched, but no one could find the girl. Then her relatives opened her grave, and found a skeleton that was much too long for the coffin. The skeleton was not wearing the clothes in which the girl had been buried. These clothes were found neatly folded and lying beside the skeleton. When the girl turned up as a zombie, she was finally caught, and sent to a convent in France. This is rather hard to believe, but her brother claimed to have visited her there.

The zombie does have some relatives. There is the dreaded *wengwa* of Gabon, in Africa. Although there are those who believe that a corpse can turn into a wengwa of its own accord, others say that it takes a sorcerer to do this. The wengwa is often described as having only one eye in the center of its forehead. And there are some who think that this ghost is a corpse by day and a were-leopard by night.

In Surinam, South America, some people believe that sorcerers are able to capture souls and use them to bring corpses back to life. Supposedly, the sorcerers can also use the captured souls to bring life to statues that are made of human flesh and placed on a wooden frame. When this happens, the result is a *bakru,* and the monster becomes the slave of the magician.

These are the stories of a few reactivated corpses found in various parts of the world. But all strange ghosts are not in human form. Many of them are animals.

FIVE / ANIMAL GHOSTS / Who ever said that ghosts are always human? Many people, all over the world, believe in animal ghosts. One such creature which is not quite a whole ghost is the hideous *srei ap* of Cambodia. It may consist of only a head and a digestive system and prowl around at night, looking for victims.

But the most common type of animal ghost seems to be man's best friend—the dog. In Lincolnshire, England, black dogs have reportedly haunted the spots where murders or suicides have occurred. They are said to have eyes that glow like hot embers.

In North Pembrokeshire, also in England, a man named David Walter was out walking his dog one night, when a huge ghostly animal appeared ahead of him. Walter commanded his dog to attack the specter, but the dog seemed frightened and did not obey. Walter's dog was not a tiny, timid animal either—it was a mastiff. Unable to get his dog to do anything, Walter picked up a stone and was

An ancient woodcut
illustrates some animal ghosts—
a donkey, a rooster, and what
appears to be a friendly dog.

about to throw it at the ghost when the evil beast suddenly disappeared in a large circle of fire.

In the Outer Hebrides Islands of Scotland, there are legends about demons that can take the shape of dogs. A story is told about a priest's dog who was sleeping near the fireplace while his master was busy hearing confessions. Imagine the priest's surprise when his dog woke up, stretched, and began to speak! The dog said, "If you liked me before, you never will again." Then he disappeared into the fireplace. The dog was never seen again.

Supposedly there was a ghostly dog that haunted Peele Castle on the Isle of Man in the Irish Sea. It was called the Manx dog, and it was seen in the shape of a spaniel. Long ago, soldiers on guard in the castle were afraid to walk down the dark passageways for fear of running into the ghost. Since none of them wanted to be alone, they began to walk in pairs.

One night, a guard who had had too much to drink began to brag. He promised that he would go alone to carry some keys to the captain of the guard. He grabbed the keys, left the guardroom, and started down a passageway. The soldiers who remained behind heard a terrible row going on outside the door. They were horrified when, a few minutes later, their drunken companion returned to the guardroom. He was struck dumb with terror, and he died in agony without ever being able to tell what had happened to him. But the soldiers knew — they believed he was killed by the Manx dog.

Legend has it that there was a human ghost, Black Vaughan, who could be found around Hergest Court in Herefordshire, England. It seems that Black Vaughan had a ghost dog who caused great mischief in the neighborhood. The stories said that the dog upset farmers' wagons and bothered travelers who were going to market. It even appeared in church one Sunday and for hours terrorized the worshippers. At other times he was content merely to wander about clanking a chain.

There is also the story about a very ambitious English weaver who died. Even after his burial he came back to his loom and was seen weaving away. He didn't harm anyone, but he was making some of the townspeople nervous. So they went to the local vicar to see what could be done about this nice, gentle ghost.

The vicar went over to the weaver's home and heard the sound of the loom coming from the upstairs room. He called to the ghost, asking him to come downstairs so that he might talk to him.

"I will," said the ghost of the weaver, "as soon as I have worked out my shuttle."

The vicar answered, "No, you have worked long enough. Come down at once."

When the ghost came down, the vicar threw a handful of churchyard dirt in his face. And immediately the ghost turned into a phantom black hound. The vicar led the dog to a neighboring pool and handed him a nutshell. He told the dog, "Take this, and dip out the pool with it. When the pool is empty, thou shalt rest."

It is said that you can still see this ghostly dog, dipping away at the pool, still unrested. Evidently, the vicar gave him a nutshell with a hole in it.

There was the Hound of Okehampton Park, in England. This dog was the ghost of a cruel English lady who lived during the thirteenth century. She was miserable to her children and was suspected of having murdered her four husbands. Anyway, it is said that she was finally condemned to run from her home to a nearby park in the form of a dog. There she was to pick one blade of grass and run back to her home with it. She was to do this over and over again until every blade of grass was gone from

Mexico has its animal ghosts.
Here the God of hunting
protects a native from one of them.

Okehampton Park. She may still be running back and forth.

Another English story is about the talking ghost dog which guards the treasure of Dobb Park Lodge. Supposedly, it is three times larger than any living dog, and will kill the treasure hunter unless he does one of three things. He must drink all of the liquor in a glass, open a chest, or draw a sword from its scabbard. Of course the tasks were harder than they sounded.

Unfortunately, the liquor turns out to be scalding hot. The chest is locked, iron-bound, and too heavy to move. And the sword keeps flying around the room so that nobody could possibly catch it.

It is said there was a phantom dog near Burnley, in England. He was called "Trash," or "Striker" by the local residents. This ghost dog had broad feet, shaggy hair, droopy ears, and eyes as large as saucers. When he walked, he made a splashing sound, as if he were walking through mud. If you tried to follow him, he would turn around and walk backwards. This way he could keep his eyes upon you.

But when he was tired of your company, he would sometimes vanish into thin air, or into a pool of water. And then all you heard was a splash. Whenever this ghost appeared, it seemed to be a sure sign that someone in the community was going to die.

Next to the dog, one of the most popular domestic animals is the cat. And there are many tales of wandering ghostly cats.

In 1838, Sir Robert Grant, governor of Bombay, died in Poona, India. On the evening of the day he died, a cat was seen leaving the Government House and walking down a path. Strangely enough, this was the same path on which the governor used to walk for exercise every evening.

For the next 25 years, the guards at the Government House followed an unwritten order to salute any cat passing out of the house after sunset. It must have been strange to see a sentry snap to attention and present arms when a cat walked by.

There was a small village near Newcastle, England, that was the home of a ghostly cat who couldn't seem to make up its mind whether to remain a cat or not. The story is a strange one. One of the serving girls in a large house noticed an unfamiliar lady in a lavender-colored dress walk past the kitchen window. This unknown woman went inside the house and up the stairs into one of the bedrooms. When the bedroom was searched, it was found empty.

Later that night, the servant's boyfriend, Thomas Davidson, came to pay a call on his sweetheart. He and his beloved decided to take a little moonlight stroll.

The ghost of a three-headed dog
seems ready to attack a god
of the Parthian religion.
The Parthians were a Middle Eastern tribe
in the first century B.C.

They were just about to start out when a white cat came out of the house and nestled down at Davidson's feet. The poor young man was obviously not a cat lover, since he tried to kick the animal away. But his foot went right through the animal's body without harming the cat in the slightest. With a flick of its tail, the cat ran off into a bush. It returned a moment later, this time in the form of a rabbit.

Much to Mr. Davidson's surprise, the rabbit hopped right up to his feet, just as the cat had done before. Once again he tried a field goal. Once again his foot went right through the animal. Once again the animal ran off behind the bush.

This time the rabbit returned as a sheep — and a shining one, at that. Davidson gave up. He stood there while the sheep came up to his feet, looked them over, and went back to the bush. Fortunately for the young man's sanity, no more animals appeared after that. But the story continues.

A clan of ghostly animals
supposedly shows the gathering reading the Black Book
in a seventeenth century print.

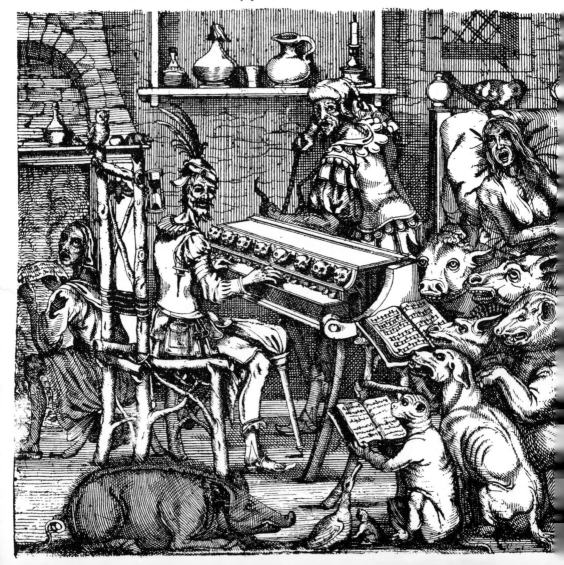

From that time on, the people who lived in the house were in for trouble. They began to hear animal noises at night. Sometimes they heard donkeys braying and galloping, cats yowling, and sheep baaing. They heard other things, too. Doors creaked, fireplace andirons fell over, and there were strange rappings all over the house. At times the lavender-gowned lady reappeared. And there were a few reports that a ghostly, bald-headed old man, dressed in a robe was also wandering around the backyard.

Another man said he saw a two-foot-high cat in one of the windows of the house. Later, a two-year-old child saw (he said) a ghost kitten. Davidson's aunt claimed that a magic handkerchief flew around in the air, but she later changed her mind and said that she had seen a ghost dog instead. Some of the children around the estate told of the fun that they had had playing with either a ghost kitten or a very strange monkey. Apparently they could not make up their minds which it was. So the family called in a kind of a fortune teller of the time — a spiritualist medium for help. But they never were able to find out what it was that was causing all the trouble.

Some believe a pig can become a ghost, too. In Denmark there is an old superstition that if you bury a live pig in a wall, it will become a ghost. It's a wonder anyone would want to bury a live pig.

There is a Scottish story that gives us an idea of how terrified some people can be of ghost pigs. Callaly Castle is located at the foot of Callaly Castle Hill. Its history is a mixture of superstition and myth. The story of why it is situated at the bottom of the hill can be found in an 1862 edition of the *Alnwick Mercury:*

"A lord of Callaly in the days of yore, commenced erecting a castle on the hill; his lady preferred a low, sheltering situation in the vale. She remonstrated, but her lord was wilful, and the building continued to progress. What she could not obtain by persuasion she sought to achieve by stratagem, and availed herself of the superstitious opinions of the age. One of her servants who was devoted to her interests, entered into her scheme: he was dressed up like a boar, and nightly he ascended the hill and pulled down all that had been built during the day. It was soon whispered that the spiritual powers were opposed to the erection of a castle on the hill; the lord himself became alarmed, and he sent some of his retainers to watch the building during the night and discover the cause of the destruction. Under the influence of the superstitions of the times those retainers magnified appearances, and when the boar issued from the wood and commenced overthrowing the work of the day, they beheld a monstrous animal of enormous power. Their terror was complete when the boar, standing among the overturned stones, cried out in a loud voice:

'Callaly Castle built on the height,
Up in the day and down in the night;
Builded down in the Shepherd's Shaw,
It shall stand for aye and never fa.'

They immediately fled and informed the lord of the supernatural visitation; and, regarding the rhymes as an expression of the will of Heaven, he abandoned the work, and, in accordance with the wish of his lady, built his castle low down in the vale where the modern mansion now stands."

Besides the pig, there are other barnyard animals that are said to come back as ghosts. There are many stories about villagers finding a strange calf in the road at night, taking it home, locking it up, and then discovering the next morning that it had disappeared.

In Shropshire, England, there is a legend about the Roaring Bull of Bagbury. This bull was a remarkable animal because it could talk. Now there was a very evil man who lived at Bagbury Farm. It was said that he only did two nice things in his entire life. One time he gave a vest to a poor man, and the other time he gave a piece of bread and some cheese to a hungry boy. That's not much of a record.

EVANSTON PUBLIC LIBRARY
CHILDREN'S DEPARTMENT
1703 ORRINGTON AVENUE
EVANSTON, ILLINOIS 60201

Very late at night
ghostly horses
were even seen
doing heavy work.

After the man died, his ghost came back in the form of a bull to haunt the farm. The roaring of this ghostly bull usually started about nine o'clock at night and continued until dawn. Soon the noise began to drive the evil man's family insane. They obviously couldn't sleep and the noise could not be ignored. So they sent for 12 parsons to see what they could do about the ghost.

When the 12 parsons arrived at the farm, they were unable to get rid of the phantom bull. So they led him away to a church. When they got him inside, all 12 parsons lit candles. But the bull began to run around so fast that the wind behind him blew out all of the candles except one. This candle was carried, oddly enough, by one of the 12 parsons who was blind. One wonders why he thought he needed a candle anyway.

While the 11 parsons were busy lighting their candles from the one that was still burning, the bull let out a roar that cracked the walls of the church. Finally they calmed the animal down and tried to decide what to do with him.

It was the bull himself who made the first suggestion. He wanted to be buried under Bagbury Bridge. But he didn't know when to stop talking, for he added that the reason he wanted that location was that if he were buried there, he could cause every pregnant woman who passed over the bridge to lose her child. And every pregnant mare would lose her foal.

Of course the parsons did not agree to this request. And, they eventually decided to kill the bull and ship it to the Red Sea where it remains buried to this day.

The horse is another farm animal which has appeared as a ghost. The story of Obrick's Colt, comes from England. A wealthy lady died and was buried wearing all of her valuable jewels. Shortly afterwards her corpse was robbed by a store clerk. This angered the lady's ghost so much that she rose from her grave in the form of a colt. The clerk's name was Obrick, and when he saw the ghostly colt, he confessed to his crime. But that did not satisfy the animal. Until the day that the store clerk died, the phantom colt pestered this man and followed him wherever he went.

Even the innocent deer and the rabbit have been reported as ghosts. There was a superstition in Cornwall, England, that if a young girl died after being betrayed by her boyfriend, she would return to haunt him in the form of a rabbit. There was once a young widow farmer who hired a beautiful girl to take charge of his dairy. They fell in love, but the farmer's family refused to let him marry the girl. She fell sick and died. Some said that afterwards, when the farmer took long walks at night, he was followed by a white rabbit.

One of the most famous of the animal ghosts is the phantom bear that was once seen in the Tower of London.

Could a toad
have become a ghost?

One night a sentry, who was on duty guarding the English Crown Jewels, saw a mist seeping under the door of the jewel chamber. The mist turned into a huge bear. Naturally, the guard lunged at it with his bayonet. But the bayonet went right through the ghost and struck the door. The sentry fell into a fit of hysterics and died three days later.

Samuel Drew, a Cornishman, had an experience with a ghostly bear. But let us hear his own words, as written down by his son:

"There were seven of us boys and men, out about 12 o'clock on a bright moonlight night. I think we were poaching. The party was in a field adjoining the road leading from my master's to St. Austell, and I was stationed outside the hedge to watch and give the alarm if any intruder should appear. While thus occupied I heard what appeared to be the sound of a horse approaching from the town, and I gave a signal.

My companions paused and came to the hedge where I was, to see the passenger. They looked through the bushes and I drew myself to the hedge that I might not be observed. The sound increased, and the supposed horseman seemed drawing near. The clatter of hoofs became more and more distinct. We all looked to see what it was, and I was seized with a strange indefinable feeling of dread: when, instead of a horse, there appeared coming towards us, at an easy pace, but with the same sound which first caught my ear, a creature about the height of a large dog. It went close by me, and as it passed, it turned upon me and my companions huge fiery eyes that struck terror to all our hearts. The road where I stood branched off and on the left there was a gate. Toward the gate the phantom moved, and without any apparent obstruction, went at its regular trot, which we heard several minutes after it had disappeared. Whatever it was, it put an end to our occupation and we made the best of our way home.

I have often endeavoured in later years, but without success, to account for what I then heard and saw on natural principles. I am sure there was no deception as to the facts. It was a night of unusual brightness, occasioned by a cloudless full moon. The creature was unlike any animal I had then seen, but from my present recollections it had much the appearance of a bear, with a dark shaggy coat. Had it not been for the unearthly lustre of its eyes, and its passing through the gate as it did, there would be no reason to suppose it anything more than an animal perhaps escaped from some menagerie. That it *did* pass through the gate without pause or hesitation I am perfectly clear. Indeed we all saw it, and saw that the gate was shut, from which we were not distant more than about 20 or 30 yards. The bars were too close to admit the passage of an animal of half its apparent bulk, yet this creature went through without an effort or variation of its pace."

Ghosts have taken the form of birds in many parts of the world. Very often, these phantoms came to warn the living of a death that was to come. Boatmen on the Bosporus, in Turkey, sometimes said that certain flocks of birds flying over the water were really the souls of the damned. They were condemned to fly forever, never to rest either on land or on water.

We cannot leave out monkey ghosts either. In 1879, a strange tale was told in Shropshire, England. A delivery man had taken some luggage from one village to another and was starting back home again. On the way, his horse became tired as they approached a small bridge. It was about ten o'clock at night, but the workman decided to stop for a while. Suddenly, a huge black creature leaped

Sometimes animal ghosts
could not make up their minds
as to which form they would take.

out of a nearby hedge and jumped on the horse's back. The workman was terrified and beat at the thing, but his whip strokes went right through the ghost. Finally, the phantom caused the horse to bolt and it raced home with the ghost still on its back.

The story was told to others and a policeman came to call on the laborer. The workman explained what had happened, and to his surprise, the policeman did not find his story strange: "Was that all? I know what that was. It was the man-monkey, sir, as *does* come at that bridge ever since a man was drowned in the canal at that spot."

All of these examples have been about ghosts which took the shapes of fairly familiar animals. But there are even stranger stories. One family in Ireland was reportedly haunted by a ghostly seal.

Some people believe in phantom hedgehogs. The *chagrin* is yet another evil spirit that some gypsies of Europe believe in. It looks like a yellow hedgehog about a foot and one-half long. The favorite sport of the chagrin

is to jump on a horse and ride it until the horse collapses. The only remedy to save the horse's life is to tie it to a stake that has been rubbed with garlic juice. Then two pieces of red thread are laid in the shape of a cross on the ground in front of the horse. Supposedly, the horse will live.

But there is a more complicated way of bringing the horse back to its senses before it dies. Mix some of the animal's hair with salt, meal, and the blood of a bat. Bake this mixture into bread and smear the bread on the hoof of the horse. Then take the pan in which the bread was baked and put it in a hole in the trunk of a tall tree. Now repeat these words:

"Tarry, pipkin, in this tree,
Till such time as full ye be."

One of the weirdest ghosts of all, however, may be the phantom fly. This tale took place in a French village near Toulon. One night, a village woman was sitting by the bedside of her sick father. The doctors had not been able to figure out what disease the old man had.

A few friends and neighbors had come over to help care for her father, but the daughter said that she would sit up with him. So the others sat in the kitchen. Later, since her father had fallen asleep, she decided to join her guests for a few minutes. No sooner had she reached the kitchen than the sick man gave out a terrible cry of pain and fright.

Everyone ran back into the bedroom only to find that a huge fly was in the room with the invalid. They tried to catch this horrible buzzing insect. But the fly was too quick for them. It not only avoided their blows, but also was able to swoop down from time to time to bite the sick man, who would then scream with pain. The bites, almost immediately, turned into black blisters and were extremely painful.

Finally one of the visitors got in a lucky shot with his hat. The fly fell to the floor and the people picked it up with a pair of fireplace tongs and threw it outside.

But the fly did not keep quiet. Its buzzing was loud enough to shake the whole house. Then a howl was heard from outside, and all became silent. The old man, of course, was still frightened, and so all of the friends and neighbors decided to spend the rest of the night sitting up with him.

The next morning they looked outside the house, and there was the huge fly lying on the ground. At least that is what they thought it was. A few of the more courageous people went over for a closer look. They reported that it was not the fly at all, but simply the outer shell of the insect. Perhaps, somewhere in France, there is an even bigger fly, lying in wait.

Goats were also popular animal spirits.
Here was one at a crossroads.

For a final look at ghostly animals, let's turn to India. In *The Sacred Books of the East,* edited by F. Max Muller, we find that unusual human beings may come back as animal ghosts.

Mortal sinners become worms or insects. Minor sinners become birds. Some criminals become aquatic animals, while others become cattle, deer, or fish. There is a wide variation, however, in the kinds of animals that common thieves can turn into.

Fish or fowl, mammal or insect, reptile or amphibian, ghosts can probably be found in almost any shape— somewhere in the world. If you look hard enough, and *if* you believe in them.

EPILOG

Good Times
& Bad Times
& all Times
get over !

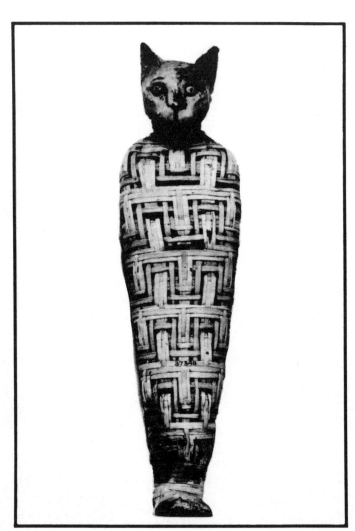

Perhaps a ghostly cat
came from this mummy case.
Its date is given as 30 B.C.

SIX / GHOSTS AND SCIENTISTS / There

are, of course, many scientific and rational explanations for these supernatural creatures. Anthropologists have studied ghosts, psychiatrists have written about apparitions, and there may even be medical explanations for them.

To begin, the belief in ghosts is as ancient as man. Anthropologists will tell us that prehistoric human bones have been found tied down to prevent them from rising out of their graves. Ancient tribes in India also believed in this custom. Other tribes in South America buried their dead head first—also to keep them from rising from their burial places.

Some tribes in Africa dug tunnels through the ground to the corpse and left food in the tunnel. This was done to prevent a future hungry corpse from rising and feeding on living people. In other parts of Africa, the dead were maimed or cut up to prevent their travels. And there was the practice of cutting off the corpse's hair; in some cultures hair was supposed to have had magical properties.

Probably the most death-conscious civilization in history was that of the Egyptians. These people believed that life continued after death in another animal form. They took great care of their dead and made mummies out of the bodies of rich people. Unfortunately, the poor people could not afford to have their relative's corpse preserved in this manner.

Nevertheless, many stories and myths have been passed down through the centuries about walking and talking mummies. Some of them are *almost* believable. Even as late as the sixth century, there were reports of people wandering into an Egyptian tomb and speaking with the entombed mummies.

Most cultures, however, were not as considerate of their dead. And so we have heard about many ghosts which were seen in the form of skeletons. No doubt these phantoms were not originally embalmed with the chemicals which would preserve their corpses.

In old Brittany, during the fourth century, some thought that if the soul did not leave the body after death, the corpse would be able to walk. The peasants there believed in the *Anaun* — the walking dead.

But what about the present — especially in Haiti? Why do some people have faith in the existence of ghosts?

The natives of this area and others like it, who believe in Voodoo, generally live a harsh and comfortless existence. Medical aid is almost nonexistent, either because it is too expensive or because the physicians are too far away. So these people have come to depend on invisible powers and spirits instead of medicine to cure their sick. Voodoo not only gives these people a way to obtain magical remedies for their illnesses, but it also gives them a chance to get together socially. No wonder the belief in Voodoo and witchcraft still exists.

There are other reasons for talking mummies and roaming vampires — psychological ones. Psychologists tell us that nearly every one of us has a hidden fear of being buried alive. Premature burial is a very real possibility. It can happen. And, indeed, it probably did happen, frequently, hundreds of years ago. There was a time when medical and mortuary sciences were not as developed as they are today. Thus, there was a greater chance for an incorrect diagnosis of death.

Consider what might have happened. A person is buried alive and then awakens. He won't live long in the grave, but before he dies he will claw and fight to get out. Later on, perhaps his neighbors dig up his grave during one of their vampire searches, and what do they find? The body's position has changed, the corpse has torn and bloody fingernails, and, very likely, scratches and blood

This old woodcut
supposedly depicts the ghost of the father
of the Duke of Buckingham
appearing at his son's deathbed.

on its face and clothing. The superstitious members of the search party might very well think that they had discovered the body of a vampire.

Or if a person had not been dead when he was buried, but rather died later, his body would not be as decomposed as the searchers might have expected. That's just one more piece of evidence for those who want to believe that a particular corpse is a vampire.

One of the reasons for premature burial was the possibility that the "dead" person was in a cataleptic trance. Catalepsy is a state in which the body becomes rigid and the affected person goes into a coma. It can be mistaken for death. The unfortunate victim is unconscious, has no will, and his normal body functions may cease. This state can last from a few minutes to several days.

A. T. Pierart was a French spiritualist who lived during the Nineteenth Century. He was one of the first people to study the problem of vampirism with the least bit of

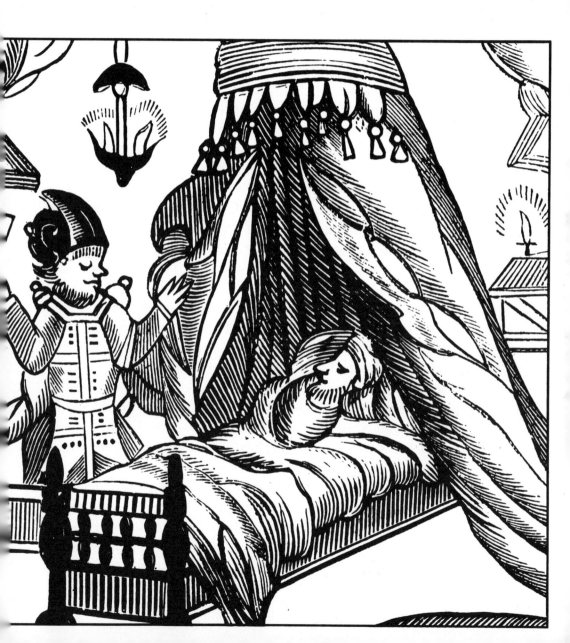

scientific curiosity. He thought that those persons whose bodies were found undecayed in their graves were really cataleptics who had been mistakenly pronounced dead.

Even if we forget the possibility of premature burial, there have been cases when a body was recovered and found undecomposed. According to religious history, there have been several saints whose bodies did not rot. There are scientific explanations for this, however. It is possible that some places of burial, either in a crypt or under the ground, are unusual. Perhaps they are places where the bacteria of decay cannot live, or perhaps they are so dry that the corpse, instead of rotting, is actually preserved.

Blood seems to be one of the most important aspects for the belief in ghosts. To find out why this liquid is so popular, we must turn to the anthropologists again. It seems that blood has always been regarded as a magical liquid. In primitive societies, there were blood sacrifices. Some tribes of American Indians drank the blood of their dead enemies. The Bible says that blood is life. And according to some religious teachings the drinking of blood from animal sacrifices was an act of faith.

Go one step further and you come up with the idea that blood might be a way to revitalize a ghost. One more step, and you can see why the superstitious people of long ago were able to blame their diseases and plagues on ghosts. As the sick person wasted away, it would be easy to say that some phantom or other had been drinking his blood.

But what about the real vampires? Yes, there have been people, although they were not ghosts, who drank blood because they were mentally sick. Psychiatrists have diagnosed these people as having been psychopaths with a special blood mania.

Those people whom psychiatrists would recognize as "vampires" may well be rather conventional appearing. For example, there was John George Haigh. He was a director of the Onslow Park Hotel in London. But he had interests other than his job. He killed nine people by luring them into his home and clubbing them to death. Then he would open their jugular veins, draw off their blood, and drink it down. After his feast, he would dissolve their bodies in sulfuric acid. He was convicted and executed in 1949.

And then there was Mary Lensfield of Brooklyn. Apparently she was a pretty woman, with pale skin, red hair, and green eyes — the last person that you would expect to be a vampire. William Seabrook, the occult writer, told of how he met her on the Riviera in 1932. They were walking along when Seabrook scraped his shoulder on a sharp rock. He said that poor Mary leaped upon him, sucking at the wound, and drank his blood.

Later she admitted her mad desire to drink blood and Seabrook was able to find a doctor who cured her.

We must, however, face one fact. The belief in vampires, zombies, and animal ghosts is not as strong in the folklore of the world as is the belief in various kinds of monsters or in witches and demons. Vampire stories seem to have been invented most often right after a piece of fiction, such as *Varney the Vampire,* appeared. Zombies have never been a really important part of the Voodoo religion. And most of the animal ghost stories were related more to witchcraft and magic than to the actual appearance of spirits. Without the *Jeepers Creepers* and *Creature Feature* television movie festivals, and without the writings of Bram Stoker and Edgar Allen Poe, who knows what part phantoms and creatures such as vampires would have played in the history of man?

ACKNOWLEDGEMENTS

pages 6–7, 10–11, 13: from *1800 Woodcuts by Thomas Bewick and His School,* Dover Publications

pages 14–15: from *Uncensored Situations,* Dick Sutphen

page 17: from *1800 Woodcuts by Thomas Bewick and His School,* Dover Publications

page 19: from the 1931 Universal picture, *Dracula;* Henry Kier Collection

page 22: Public Domain

page 25: from *Varney the Vampire* by Thomas Preskett Prest

page 28: from a sixteenth century engraving

page 32: New York Public Library Picture Collection, parts of this painting appear on pages 1–5

page 33: from *1800 Woodcuts by Thomas Bewick and His School,* Dover Publications

pages 34–35: sources unknown

page 36: from *Man, Myth and Magic,* by M. Boyd, Criterion

page 41: New York Public Library Picture Collection

page 43: from *The Supernatural,* by Hill and Williams, Hawthorne

page 51: from *1800 Woodcuts by Thomas Bewick and His School,* Dover Publications

page 53: 1720 woodcut, source unknown

page 61: source unknown

pages 66–67: from *Man, Myth and Magic,* by M. Boyd, Criterion pages 72–73: source unknown

page 74: from *1800 Woodcuts by Thomas Bewick and His School,* Dover Publications

page 77: from a seventeenth century print, artist unknown

pages 79–81: native artists unknown

page 85: from *1800 Woodcuts by Thomas Bewick and His School,* Dover Publications

page 87: from De Laniis et Philtonicis Mulieribus, by Ulrich Molitor, 1490

pages 90–91, 95: source unknown

page 96: woodcut by Franz van der Wyngaert, seventeenth century

pages 100–101: from a nineteenth century print, artist unknown

page 104: etching by Johannes de Cuba 1498

page 109: etching by Sebastian Munster, 1544

page 113: from *La Poule Noire,* artist unknown, 1820

pages 114–115: from *1800 Woodcuts by Thomas Bewick and His School,* Dover Publications

page 116: from the British Museum

page 117: from *1800 Woodcuts by Thomas Bewick and His School,* Dover Publications

page 121: source unknown

INDEX

ABOUT THE AUTHOR / Once again Thomas Aylesworth explores the unknown worlds of science and superstition. This time his skilled pen concentrates on the familiar but rarely discussed subjects of vampires and ghosts.

Since earning his Ph.D. from Ohio State University, Thomas G. Aylesworth has been an assistant professor at Michigan State University, and Senior Editor of Current Science. Presently, Dr. Aylesworth is Senior Editor at Doubleday and Company and The Natural History Press.

The author of numerous books since 1964, some of these titles are: IT WORKS LIKE THIS; LOOK INTO THE FUTURE; THIS VITAL AIR, THIS VITAL WATER; and TRAVELING INTO TOMORROW. Other Addisonian Press titles written by the author include, SERVANTS OF THE DEVIL, and WEREWOLVES AND OTHER MONSTERS. Although he is an extremely busy and prolific writer, Dr. Aylesworth still finds time for sailing or playing tennis.